LIFE AND BATTLES

OF

James J. CORBETT.

PRICE 25¢

RICHARD K. FOX
PUBLISHER
FRANKLIN SQUARE NEW YORK CITY.

BOOKS YOU SHOULD READ.

SENSATIONAL BOOKS.

GLIMPSES OF GOTHAM; or, New York by Day light and after Dark.

MAN TRAPS OF NEW YORK. A Full Expose of the Metropolitan Swindler.

NEW YORK BY DAY AND NIGHT. A Continuation of Glimpses of Gotham.

NEW YORK TOMBS; its Secrets, Romances, Crimes and Mysteries.

MYSTERIES OF NEW YORK UNVEILED. One of the most exciting books publi-hed.

PARIS BY GASLIGHT. The Gay Life of the Gayest City in the World.

PARIS INSIDE OUT; or, Joe Potts on the Loose. A Vivid St ry of Parisian Life.

SECRETS OF THE STAGE; or, the Mysteries of the Play House Unveiled.

GREAT ARTISTS OF THE AMERICAN STAGE. Portraits of the Actors and Actresses of America.

CONEY ISLAND FROLICS. How New York's Gay Girls and Jolly Boys Enjoy Themselves by the Sea.

HISTORY OF THE WHITECHAPEL MURDERS.

MABILLE UNMASKED; or the Wickedest Place in the World.

BELLA STARR. The Bandit Queen of the West. Her Daring Exploits and Adventures.

ADVENTURESS EVA; or, the Wiles of Wicked Woman. The Life and Adventures of Mrs. Robert Ray Hamilton.

THE HANGING OF THE CHICAGO ANARCHISTS. Illustrated History of Anarchy in America.

BILLY LEROY, THE COLORADO BANDIT. The King of American Highwaymen.

MYSTERIES OF MORMONISM. A Full Expose of its Hidden Crimes.

LIVES OF THE POISONERS. The most Fascinating book of the year.

FOLLY'S QUEENS; or, Women Whose Love Ruled the World.

FOOTLIGHT FAVORITES. Portraits of the Leading American and European Actresses.

SUICIDE'S CRANKS; or, the Curiosities of Self-Murder. Showing the Origin of Suicide.

JAMES BROTHERS, THE CELEBRATED OUTLAW BROTHERS. Their Lives and Adventures.

PARIS UNVEILED. Expose of Vice and Crime in the Gay French Capital.

HISTORIC CRIMES. A Graphic History of Startling and Mysterious Crimes.

SPORTING BOOKS.

THE AMERICAN ATHLETE. A Treatise on the Principles and Rules of Training.

CHAMPIONS OF THE AMERICAN PRIZE RING. Complete History and Portraits of all the American Heavy-weights.

"POLICE GAZETTE" STANDARD BOOK OF RULES. Revised and Corrected.

THE COCKER'S GUIDE. Contains everything about Game Fowls.

BOXING AND HOW TO TRAIN.

THE CHAMPIONS OF ENGLAND.

"POLICE GAZETTE" CARD PLAYER. All desired Information.

THE BARTENDERS' GUIDE.

LIFE OF JOHN L. SULLIVAN. Champion of the World.

LIFE OF JAKE KILRAIN, Ex-Champion of the World.

LIFE OF TUG WILSON, Champion Pugilist of England.

LIFE OF TOM SAYERS.

LIVES OF TOM HYER, JOHN C. HEENAN, YANKEE SULLIVAN AND JOHN MORRISSEY. Complete in one volume.

LIFE OF JACK DEMPSEY, Champion Middle Weight of the World.

THE ART OF WRESTLING.

THE DOG PIT. How to Select and Train Fighting Dogs.

Any of the above Illustrated Books sent by mail on receipt of **25 cents.**

Full History of the Sullivan-Kilrain Fight in book form. 15 cents.

The Terrible Johnstown Disaster in book form. Profusely Illustrated. Price 15 cents.

MISCELLANEOUS SPORTING BOOKS.

The American Hoyle	$2 00	American Card Player		5
Games of Patience	75 1 00	How Gamblers Win	30,	5
Poker Player	50 1 00	One Hundred Tricks with Cards	30,	5
Hand Book of Wist	25	Art of Gymnastics		1 0
New Card Games	26	Dumbbell and Indian Club Exercises		2
Procto 's Draw Poker	15	Art of Wrestling		2
Hoyle's Games	50, 75, 1 00	Art of Attack and Defence		2
Hand Book of Cribbage	50	Donnelley's Art of Boxing		2
Progressive Poker	25	The Science of Self Defense		2
Pocket Hoyle	50, 75, 1 00	Boxing Made Easy		1
Book on Draughts	1 50	Modern Bartenders' Guide		1
American Draught Players	3 00	Beale's Calisthenics for Young Folks	1 0
Draughts f r Beginners	75	Billy Edwards Art of Boxing		7
Manual of Chess	50	Art of Training Animals		6

RICHARD K. FOX, Publisher, Franklin Square, N. Y.

LIFE AND BATTLES

OF

JAMES J. CORBETT

— THE —

Champion Pugilist of the World.

ILLUSTRATED.

New York:

RICHARD K. FOX, PUBLISHER, FRANKLIN SQUARE.

1892.

PREFACE.

IN order that the thousands interested in pugilism in both hemispheres, who have read or heard how James J. Corbett of San Francisco won the prize ring championship of the World, in a contest for $10,000 a side and a purse of $25,000 offered by the now historic Olympic Club, of New Orleans, La., may read a graphic description of the big battle and also know something about the champion of the world in 1892, Richard K. Fox has decided to publish the book entitled the "Life and Battles of James J. Corbett, the Champion Pugilist of the World."

The book is illustrated and contains complete reports of Corbett's defeat of Jake Kilrain; his drawn battle for $10,000 with Peter Jackson, the Black Demon, and his historic encounter with John L. Sullivan, who had held the title from 1882 to 1886 and from 1889 to 1892 without ever meeting with defeat.

Owing to the fact that there are millions who did not see the great contest between Corbett and Sullivan on Sept. 7, 1892, in New Orleans, the book will no doubt be read with considerable interest and will be kept as a reference.

THE AUTHOR.

RICHARD K. FOX

Editor and Proprietor of the "Police Gazette" and "Fox's
Illustrated Weekly."

DONOR OF THE POLICE GAZETTE HEAVY, MIDDLE, LIGHT AND
FEATHER-WEIGHT PRIZE RING CHAMPIONSHIP BELTS, THE
CHAMPIONSHIP CHALLENGE ROWING CUP AND THE SIX-
DAY GO-AS-YOU-PLEASE CHAMPIONSHIP BELT
OF THE WORLD, ETC., ETC., VALUED
AT OVER $100,000.

INTRODUCTION.

SINCE Tom Hyer, an American, born on February 7, 1849, won the Prize Ring Championship of America at Still Pond, Maryland, there never has been such a good-looking and gentlemanly champion as James J. Corbett, of San Francisco, Cal., better known in prize ring circles as the California Wonder. Corbett is not only blessed with a pleasing countenance, but stripped in condition ready for the fray, he would be a great study for a sculptor, his form being of the Apollo order, while his physical development is grand, and clearly demonstrates the benefits derived from early training and regular athletic exercises.

As a boxer Corbett is a professor. He displays all the superior requisites of the science of the manly art of self-defence. His attitude is manly, and even in the most trying moments of a battle his postures are graceful.

His intellectual attainments have made it possible for him to familiarize himself with the human frame. His habits of life and his early education tended to make him a prominent figure in social and professional walks of life. He is essentially a gentleman, and has made hosts of friends.

JAMES J. CORBETT, CHAMPION PUGILIST OF THE WORLD.

LIFE AND BATTLES OF JAMES J. CORBETT.

CHAPTER I.

CORBETT'S EARLY LIFE.

Patrick J. Corbett sailed from Ireland to New Orleans in 1854. Not being as prosperous there as he wished, and hearing much of the "glorious climate of California," he concluded to betake himself to the Golden Gate and settle th re. About three years after his arrival there he married, and nine children are the result of the union. The family consists of Frank, Harry, James J., Thomas, Joseph, Esther, Theresa, Kate and Mary. The third of the boys, whose full name is James John Corbett, was born September 1, 1866. He is now in his twenty-seventh year, and is the holder of the proud title "Champion Pugilist of the World," which he won by his game and complete defeat of the erstwhile idol of the pugilistic world, the mighty and hitherto invincible John Lawrence Sullivan, of Boston.

Master Corbett was a pretty steady attendant of the Sacred Heart College, San Francisco, although his love for the game of fisticuffs caused his parents and teachers many an anxious hour, and his willingness to thump and be thumped was the principal characteristic of his early years. He himself describes a fight with a schoolmate as one of the hardest battles of his life. He said recently:

"I had rather fight in the ring than out of it any time. One of the hardest bouts I ever had in my life was when I was fourteen years of age. I was attending St. Ignatius' College at the time. There were two yards at this college, called the 'big yard' and the 'little yard.' When pupils reached a certain degree of proficiency they were promoted from the little to the big yard. Dave Egan, my chum, and myself had just been promoted and did not know many of the fellows over the fence. We chipped into their games just the same and soon got acquainted. At that time 'Fatty' Carney, a big, burly boy, was the recognized bully of the yard. He had an unpleasant habit of putting heads on people who looked cross-eyed at him. I had never made any name for myself as a fighting boy and did not want to.

"One day we were playing 'prisoners' base.' Carney was not in the game, but he took deliberate pains to run into my chum Egan. We had a few words and he got dead sore on me. 'I'll tend to you after school,' said he.

"After school was out one of my friends came to me and said, 'Fatty Carney is laying for you outside and is going to lick you.' I was terribly afraid at first and was going to run home, but something stopped me. I don't know what it was—pride, maybe. Anyway I sallied out and found Carney waiting for me with his coat off. I walked right up to him and asked what he wanted 'I'm goin' ter lick yer out of your boots,' he replied. I hauled off my coat without a word and we went over to a vacant lot.

"I had no more idea of sparring than a hog nas of Christmas. I had seen one fellow spar, however, and had noticed him looking at his opponent's stomach and hitting for his face. I did the same thing to Fatty and was overjoyed at the result. The longer we fought the more enthusiastic I became. I was not angry ; I was simply delighted with the scrap. I had him almost pounded out, when there came a wild cry of police. Fatty sifted and I sifted in the same direction. We went up to another open lot and got at it again. I was getting the better of it when he started in on a rough and tumble.

"He was bigger and stronger than I and he was rapidly doing me up when a man with a gold-headed cane interfered. He pulled Fatty off, stood us both up and said: 'Now go at him and if he does not fight fair I'll warm him with this cane.' It was a long fight, but I licked him at last, and went home tired out.

"The next day the president of the college called me up

MIKE DONOVAN, CORBETT'S ADVISER,

PROF. DONALDSON.

before the throne and asked me where I got the bruised eye. 'Me and Fatty Carney had a fight,' I replied. 'Who licked!' he asked. I told him all about it and he fired us both out of school. That fight gave me quite a reputation among my school-mates.

"Afterwards I used to box in my father's stable. Every stable hand who came there for employment had to put on the gloves with me. There was one fellow around there called 'Forty' Kenealy, who was a rather tough nut in the boxing line. One day Kenealy and I were present at an entertainment given by the Sullivan Cadets. The president of the cadets seeing us both present got up and asked us for a bout. 'Will you box?' asked Kenealy. 'Yes,' I replied, 'come on.' We got at it and a regular slugging match followed. He was a hard customer, and for a time it was about even up. Finally he swung out at me and I ducked. As I came up my head struck him in the chin and almost knocked him out. Everybody thought I had hit him with my fist, and Kenealy thought so himself. When they stopped us he was all but gone."

Like his late antagonist, Corbett's first idea when he had passed his boyhood years was to become a professional baseball player. He played with the amateur nines around San Francisco and became quite proficient as a ball-tosser. He was bent on emulating Anson, Joe Start, John Morrill, Burdock and others who were the baseball heroes of the boys of those days. A position was offered him, however, in the Nevada National Bank, and in compliance with the earnest wishes of his mother and the very strongly expressed sentiments of his father he dropped baseball and became an assistant bookkeeper in the bank, which position he held for several years. But to this day the champion is a great admirer of the national game and a personal friend of most of the prominent players.

As soon as he was able to know and appreciate the benefits of gymnastic exercises, Jim joined the Olympic Athletic Club, of his native city, and quickly became proficient. Particularly was he fond of boxing, and constant practice under Prof. Walter Watkins, whose principal idea of boxing is to counter rather than to ward off blows, soon made him the superior of any amateur heavy-weight who entered the tournaments of the club. He won the championship competitions at least half a dozen times before his eighteenth year.

Every professional that came to San Francisco and visited the club-rooms Jim was anxious to put on the gloves with, and finding that he held his own with nearly all of them he determined to become a professional fighter.

CHAPTER II.

CORBETT BECOMES A FIGHTER.

In 1884 he made his debut as a full-fledged knight of the knuckles. His first professional engagement was with Dave Eisemann, and Corbett disposed of him very handily in two rounds. He next defeated Duncan McDonald, of Butte, Mont., in four rounds. In regard to his meetings with Choynski, of San Francisco, Corbett says :

"There has been much discussion relative to my meetings with Choynski. I'll tell you all about it. My brother and Choynski's were both employed in the City Hall. One day they became involved in an argument respecting our relative abilities. Up to this time I had never seen Choynski. The result of this argument was that Choynski's brother brought him to my father's barn and I stopped him in one round. After that Choynski began to box with professionals. He also circulated the report that I could box, but could not fight. We made a match to fight in private in the old familiar barn on a Sunday. When the time came fully five thousand persons, who had received 'quiet' tips on the event, were parading up and down in front of my father's house. The family were greatly disturbed and my father persuaded me not to fight. He gave me an awful talk. 'I'll go up and tell him I won't fight,' said I.

"I went to Choynski's house and his brother came to the door. Before I had a chance to say anything he said : 'Oh, he'll be there quick enough. You need not be anxious.' This made me mad and I told him to trot out his brother and I would fight him anyway.

"Choynski came out and we walked ten miles over t

JOE CHOYNSKI.

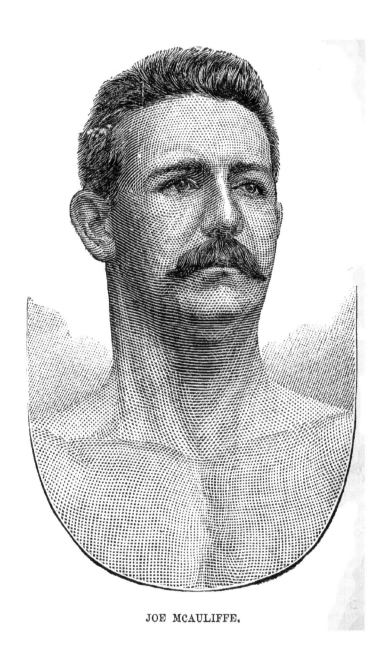

JOE MCAULIFFE.

the sand hills and went at it with bare knuckles. I knocked him out in two rounds and then went over and punched his brother in the nose. The next time we fought was at the Olympic Club a year afterward. He had been blowing again about how he could lick me. On this occasion I knocked him out the very first pass I made at him. After he got up I said : 'Now, I'll make the set-to a friendly one if you want it that way.' Pretty soon he got fresh, and I had to knock him out again."

The last time these young men came together was on a barge on the Sacramento River. Choynski was seconded by that great ring general, Jack Dempsey, and made a game and determined stand against Corbett. The latter broke his hand on Joe, but won in twenty-seven rounds. Between his fights with Choynski, Jim filled in the chinks by fighting with and defeating a number of ambitious heavy-weights. Up to his fight with a man of tremendous strength and stature named Mike Brennan and known as the "Port Costa Giant," whom Corbett easily defeated, despite the great difference in weight and height, many San Francisco sports had sneered at Jim's professional aspirations and predicted his early downfall. But when this mighty man of brawn went down before the gentlemanly young boxer many of the doubting Thomases began to change their tune and to think there might be something in the young Olympic Club athlete after all.

Before Corbett entered his nineteenth year Jack Burke, the Irish lad, came to San Francisco. Burke had boxed with Sullivan, Mitchell and Dempsey, and was quite a pugilistic star. He and Corbett boxed eight rounds and the bout was declared a draw. This encouraged him and his friends greatly, as Burke was considered a foeman worthy of almost anybody's fists.

Corbett defeated in rapid succession Capt. James Daly, in two rounds ; Frank Smith, of Salt Lake, in three ; George Atkinson, in two, and Frank Glover, the well-known Chicago heavy-weight, in two. Then came his last fight with Choynski on the barge

He next met Joe McAuliffe, who was considered by many the coming heavy-weight champion. They met in a four-round contest for points and Corbett easily got the decision. About this time Jim accepted an offer of a position as boxing instructor of the Olympic Club and confined himself closely to business, finding time, however, to do up a few more heavy-weights who thought him a soft mark. Prof. John Donaldson, who has since seconded Jim against Jackson and Sullivan, was one of these deluded individuals and was easily defeated by Corbett.

Prof. William Miller, now of Australia, was at one time a prominent figure in athletics in New York. He was teacher of wrestling in the short-lived Police Athletic Club, and wrestled Bauer in the Græco-Roman style all night long to a draw at Gilmore's Garden. The Professor arrived in San Francisco on his travels, went up before Corbett and met the usual fate. He was easily defeated in three rounds. This victory put Corbett's stock away up in his native city, and his admirers were now numbered by thousands.

He went to Portland, Ore., and easily defeated Dave Campbell, of that city, who was considered a comer. Corbett's next fight was the one he considers the most important in his career.

CHAPTER III.

CORBETT'S BATTLE WITH KILRAIN.

In February, 1890, hearing that Jake Kilrain was in New Orleans with Muldoon's combination of boxers Corbett went to that city and endeavored to get on a "go" with the Baltimorean. It was during his stay at New Orleans that he was visited by Phil Dwyer, the well-known turfman of Brooklyn, who had heard of the young Californian's prowess and admired him greatly. He introduced himself to Corbett, who said: "Mr. Dwyer I have heard of you ever since I can remember, and knowing what your standing is among sporting men I am obliged to you for coming to see me." Dwyer was much impressed by Corbett's gentlemanly demeanor and told him he would be glad to be of any assistance to him. He said to Corbett:

"I suppose you are aware that you are going up against a pretty hard game with this man Kilrain," to

JAKE KILRAIN.

FRANK GLOVER.

which Jim replied : "I will beat him and beat him very fast, I know what I can do and when you see us come together you will be surprised."

Corbett and Kilrain finally arranged to fight a six-round glove contest for a purse of $3,500 before the Southern Athletic Club. They met Feb. 17, 1890. There was a big crowd present.

Unusual interest was manifested in the affair, and at the pool rooms and at the club and sporting resorts there was brisk speculation on the result, Kilrain being the favorite at 2 to 1.

The Southern Athletic Club had provided two other contests besides the Kilrain and Corbett match. One was between George Bezinah, of Covington, Ky., who killed James, at Dallas, Tex., and Charley Johnson of New Orleans, and Mike E. Smith, of Cincinnati, and Mike Cleary, of New York. These contests preceded the more important one and did not last long. In the Cleary and Smith battle the New York pugilist surprised the natives by knocking out his muscular opponent in the second round. Smith stopped a right hand cross-counter on the jaw which made him drop as if he was shot. Cleary was loudly cheered for the quick off-hand way in which he put the Cincinnati pugilist to sleep.

The contest between Bezinah and Johnson lasted four rounds, and Bezinah won easily.

After these contests the ring was cleared and everything was made ready for Corbett and Kilrain to fight. Corbett entered the ring weighing 183 pounds. Kilrain weighed 201 pounds, six pounds less than when he knocked out Vacquelin.

Kilrain had Muldoon and Cleary behind him, while Corbett was seconded by Tommy Danforth and Mike Smith, while George Scott was bottle holder. Muldoon introduced the men, and announced that Kilrain weighed 201 pounds. Corbett looked over at his burly rival and said incredulously : "Then you can put me down for 170 pounds."

E. R. Violet, the well-known cotton man and an enthusiastic amateur sparrer, was selected by the Club as referee, and A. M. Hill and R. A. Fox, timers. Then time was called without any more preliminaries and both men sprang lightly forward to the scratch, Corbett smiling as if eager for the fray. Both men sparred for an opening, watching each other's style, for it was the first time they had met.

Corbett carried his left loosely, while his right held guard.

The fight was a lively one until round 6, when Corbett led with his left and found Kilrain's head. The latter responded with a blow in the breast and Corbett countered heavily on the stomach. Kilrain found Corbett's wind with his left and repeated the blows. Corbett meanwhile paid his attention to the Baltimorean's head and ribs, landing both blows. Kilrain then rushed for the ribs and neck and Corbett found his wind once more.

Kilrain played for Corbett's stomach with his left, but the blow was a little slow and Corbett's left went out hard and straight and caught Kilrain on the nose. It was a hard rap and made the Champion wince. Kilrain rushed again and landed his left on the chest and his right on Corbett's neck, clinching again as time was called.

The fight was over and the crowd was all one way. There were shouts of "Corbett! Corbett!" and Corbett was as happy as a schoolboy in his corner. Kilrain came forward and claimed that only five rounds had been fought, but the tally showed six, and Referee Violet announced that, as the fight was to be decided on scientific points and not on strength of blows, he awarded the victory to Corbett. Corbett received an ovation and was almost carried to his dressing room by his admirers.

Prior to Corbett's victory over Kilrain he was not known outside of the Pacific Slope, but the fact that he had defeated Kilrain, who had fought Jem Smith, the Champion of England, a draw for $10,000 and the POLICE GAZETTE championship belt, fought John L. Sullivan seventy-five rounds according to London prize ring rules for $22,000, gave Corbett a world-wide reputation, and he was feted and banqueted. Many looked upon him as a rising pugilistic star.

Shortly after his victory over Kilrain Corbett came to New York. . He was the guest of Prof. Mike Donovan, the instructor in boxing of the New York Athletic Club.

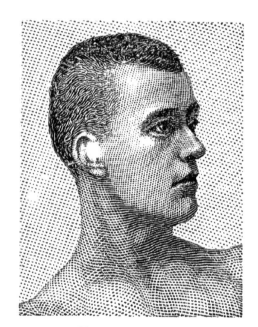

JOHNNY REAGAN.

DOMINICK McCAFFREY.

Donovan brought Corbett to the POLICE GAZETTE office where he was photographed, and a large portrait was published in that paper. Corbett was then introduced in the New York Athletic Club and his gentlemanly manners gained him a legion of friends.

Corbett was then matched against Dominick McCaffrey, a pugilist who had fought John L. Sullivan and other noted ring men.

CHAPTER IV.

CORBETT'S BATTLE WITH McCAFFREY.

The encounter between Corbett and McCaffrey, for gate money, was brought off at the Casino, Brooklyn, N. Y., on the evening of April 14, 1890. About 2,500 persons journeyed to witness the affair, and among the crowd were many well-known in the sporting, social and financial world. Among the crowd were Big John Quinn, Phil Dwyer, Matt Corbett, Jim Barclay, Jimmy Patterson, Prof. Mike Donovan, Lon Ackerman, George Engeman. Charley Johnston and John Kelly, while the fistic brigade was well represented. It was after 10 o'clock when the gladiators entered the arena. Corbett occupied the northwest corner, while McCaffrey made the south-eastern corner of the ring his headquarters.

Neither was attended by seconds, nor were there official time-keepers or referee. The rounds were to be three minutes each and one minute rest between each, otherwise POLICE GAZETTE rules governed. The rules were not adhered to, however. If they had been Corbett would no doubt have ended the struggle in the third round.

In the first round McCaffrey showed to advantage, but there was none of that quick dash and agility he used to display, and one of Corbett's straight left-handers on the mark twisted him like a rainbow. A few exchanges and a clinch, in which McCaffrey hung to Corbett like a barnacle to a ship's bottom, and time was called amid yells and hisses and shouts of "That is not three minutes!"

The second round was a repetition of the first. Corbett doing the smashing and McCaffrey doing the hugging.

It was plain to be seen that the California Wonder was the master of the situation, and could, by a straight left-hand blow followed by a right-hand cross-counter, have ended the contest, but, strange to say, he did not attempt to do so, but only banged McCaffrey whenever the latter stood up to him.   McCaffrey tried to dodge, jostle and hang on to Corbett, and time was again called after the men had been been battling two minutes.   The crowd, who had paid $1 and $2, now began to yell that the rounds were short, and, to appease the excitement, Johnny Reagan jumped on the stage to keep time.

In the third round there was hardly any feinting as the men came to the centre.   Corbett let go and caught McCaffrey a staggerer on the nose.   Mac's counters failed to reach, and twice more the Californian's left found a resting place.   Mac's nose was trickling with blood, but he did not sail in.   McCaffrey recovered and got in on Corbett's face lightly.   Corbett settled down to his work and got decidedly the best of the long-range shots.   Mac seemed to grow suddenly tired and weakened under Corbett's hammering.   Mac landed on Corbett's nose with his left, but was heavily cross-countered and two more efforts of McCaffrey's to land were futile.   The round ended in Mac's corner.

As soon as they faced each other McCaffrey led with his left, but was severely countered.   Corbett rushed his man to the ropes and tried upper-cutting, but McCaffrey clinched skillfully.   Corbett broke away and got in both right and left heavily, and McCaffrey was weakening fast. Corbett banged McCaffrey into his corner and out of it, and then fought him to the ropes.   Either from weakness or in attempting to avoid punishment, McCaffrey bent over the ropes.   With an effort he turned his face toward his opponent as though to look if anything more was coming, but Corbett had stepped back and thrown up his hands in an appeal to Steve O'Donnell to excuse him from doing any more dama e.   Steve said he guessed that would do, and seriously declared that "Mr. Corbett had the best of the bout."

Corbett then returned to San Francisco, Cal., and after a brief rest he once more resumed his old position of boxing

STEVE O'DONNELL.

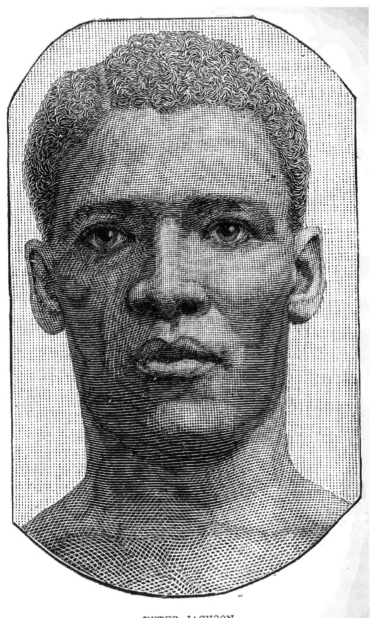

PETER JACKSON,

instructor in the Olympic Amateur Athletic Club.

Corbett's ambition was to become champion of America and later in the summer of 1890 he issued a challenge to fight any man in the world for $5,000 a side. At this time Peter Jackson was about to return from Australia, and the California Athletic Club decided to bring about a match between Corbett and Jackson on the latter's return.

CHAPTER V.

THE CHAMPION'S BATTLE WITH PETER JACKSON.

In 1890 Peter Jackson, the Black Demon, the greatest colored pugilist who ever stepped in a prize ring, was challenged by Corbett to meet him in the orthodox twenty-four foot ring. The Black Demon picked up the gauntlet and the California Athletic Club offered a purse of $10,000 for Corbett and Jackson to fight for.

The match, after it was arranged, created considerable interest in England, Australia and America, and owing to the fact that Jackson had quite a fistic record he was made a heavy favorite and thousands of dollars were wagered on the re-ult.

The battle was decided on May 21 and 22, 1891. It was claimed that both men were in the "pink of condition" when they entered the ring and the friends of each were confident that their favorite would punch his way to victory. The gladiators were cautious and apparently afraid that the other might obtain an advantage. Very little hard hitting was done at the start, Corbett clinching on every occasion to avoid punishment, it would appear. A great deal of science was displayed, and Jackson succeeded in drawing first blood. Toward the close the men fought more viciously, and the Californian landed some powerful blows upon his opponent's body and head. They would have knocked out an ordinary man, but the negro seemed to be made of tough material. It was anybody's fight to the last. Both men were severely punished and completely exhausted. At the wind up of the sixty-first round they were physically unfit to continue, and the referee decided the battle a draw.

The following are the details of the battle :

Peter Jackson's seconds were Sam Fitzpatrick, who has stood behind him in all his battles, and Billy Smith, with Billy Fields, who gave Jackson the use of his forge in training, as bottleholder. Corbett was served by John Donaldson and Billy Delaney, with his brother, Harry Corbett, as bottleholder. Hiram Cook, who has refereed all the big fights at the club, acted as referee.

After two preliminary scraps the main event was called. Both men appeared shortly before 9 o'clock. Jackson weighed 197 pounds and Corbett 185. The betting just before the men entered the ring was 2 to 1 on Jackson. It had been 10 to 6 all the afternoon.

The following is a description of the fight by rounds :

ROUND 1—On the gong sounding both men promptly walked to the centre, exchanged the usual hand-shaking formalities and the fight began. There was considerable sparring, when Jackson tried that old left-hand body jab and failed to get in, but Corbett was most uncomfortably awkward in getting away. This gauged his speed, and, as though acknowledging his weakness, he clinched the next moment. Two lovers never hugged so closely. Jackson tried hard enough to get away, but Corbett wouldn't have it. Hiram Cook, the referee, stepped in and separated them. Corbett made a left swing, failed to get in, and Jackson hit him hard with a straight right-hander under the heart.

ROUND 2—At the opening of this round Corbett jumped to the centre, but it was plain to see his heart was not in the jump, so he jumped away again, the Australian following him like a cat. A clinch followed, but both hugged, and no harm was done. Jackson, after the breakaway, pursued the Californian about the ring and Corbett, turning, engaged him at close quarters. It was another hugging match, and in the breakaway Corbett tried a vicious left swing which barely missed Jackson's jaw. Corbett landed two or three light ones on the body before the call of time.

ROUND 3—Jackson landed his right on Corbett's heart. Corbett's left was in working order, however, and Jackson retreated before a heavy blow. Corbett followed the re-

JACKSON RUSHES.

CORBETT LANDS ON JACKSON'S JAW.

treating steps of his opponent, who, when the opportunity showed itself, paid absolutely no attention to the dusky man's head, but went diligently to work on his wind. If there is anything Jackson seems to hate to have interfered with it is his stomach, and while stretching out his length to injudicious counters he threw his body back out of all danger. Corbett's hugging tactics were not greeted with any marked degree of appreciation by the audience, but in the wind-up of the round his clever ducking from straight left-hand jabs gained him much applause.

ROUND 4—This was a well contested round, so far as sparring was concerned, but little damage was done on either side. Toward the end Corbett landed three good hot ones on the negro's jaw with his left hand, and then, seeming to gain confidence, followed his man and shot in a few more straight-arm lefts on Jackson's body and jaw. The spectators went wild at this slight change in favor of the white man, but Jackson kept on smiling that wicked smile.

ROUND 5—Jackson assumed the aggressive at the opening and there was a clinch immediately after the negro's lead. · At the break Corbett found it necessary to seek refuge at a distance, Jackson giving him a blow over the heart. Jackson's good-natured face was wide open with a grin, which belied a horrible straight right he delivered the next minute. Corbett seemed to be the receiver generally up to this point of the affray, which was beginning to look anything else but like the great scientific set-to that was expected.

ROUND 6—Jackson at once assumed the aggressive, however, and kept following Corbett around the ring Corbett kept out of harm's way cleverly enough, though, and occasionally parried things by turning and poking his left at Jackson's wind. As the bell struck Corbett got in a good left-hand swing on the Australian's jaw. In the interim between the sixth and seventh rounds the lump of ice rubbed on Jackson's head diminished half its size. There was a speck of blood, too, on his breeches, but not enough to be traced to either.

ROUND 7—In this round there was no damage done on either side, but Jackson was nearly blinded by the perspiration that was falling off his receding brow.

ROUND 8—Both displayed careful tactics during half of this round, and then suddenly showed bursts of speed. A hot rally in the centre of the ring followed, in which Corbett evened things up. Jackson nearly jerked his arm out trying to reach him with his left and later landed another blow on Corbett's jaw. A clinch followed and the round ended.

ROUND 9—This round opened viciously enough, as though each man thought the other personally responsible for the apparently short space of time in which he was allowed to rest. Corbett got away again most cleverly from Jackson's threatening left jab, and after a clinch and a little in-fighting they broke away seemingly unharmed. Hardly had a second passed before Corbett's left-arm swing came as suddenly and unexpectedly as possible, finding Jackson's jaw unprotected. It was a terrible smash, under which the Australian quailed more than under any other blow he has ever received before an American audience. The round closed before much could be done.

ROUND 10—Corbett led first, and Jackson returned the compliment by half a dozen nasty short-arm jabs in the wind. After a breakaway Jackson sent several right and left swings at Corbett's head, but the latter cleverly ducked away, saving his jaw and earning cheers from the spectators. Jackson visited the Californian's stomach good and hard just at the call of time.

ROUND 11—Corbett, after a feint, got in his favorite swing on Jackson's wind, and the shouting was ear-splitting. This was cut short in the next pass, and Jackson's ugly left did some execution, under which Corbett winced. In this round more than any other so far Corbett showed he really was a clever sparrer, repeatedly, like an active catamount, escaping Jackson's left. Corbett's head was either to the right or left of Jackson's fist each time, while his hands were busily engaged playing a tattoo on Jackson's ribs.

ROUND 12—Jackson managed to land his left on Corbett's jaw, which must have severely jostled his anatomy for some moments. Corbett got savage on Jackson's wind and honors were again nearly equal. Fierce exchanges with no harm done ended the round.

PAT DUFFY.

WALTER WATSON.

ROUND 13—This was a desperate round and was made up with the most offensive punches of the evening, except in the last thirty seconds, during which Jackson followed his man up along the ropes from corner to corner, occasionally reminding him of the trouble he was in with left-handers.

ROUND 14—The Australian was on the aggressive, but he wasted fully as much force in pursuing Corbett as the latter did in escaping his vicious onslaughts. He got one good one on Corbett's heart, though he received only a light return for it. Corbett landed on the jaw, but the visitation was without force, owing to weakness, wh ch was becoming apparent in both men. It was seen that both were certainly masters as near as could be of the manly art of self defence, if not of the other's destruction.

ROUND 15—Both pugilists showed how careful each was of the other's welfare by stopping, ha ds down, while Corbett turned his back to Jackson and kicked out of the ring a cork that had fallen from a soda water bottle.

ROUND 16 was wasted in fiddling away at a safe distance. Then Corbett shot out his left, getting a good one on Jackson's wind. He got in a good right-hander the next minute, which landed with terrific force on Jackson's jaw. The crowd yelled and Corbett, taking new heart, crowded Jackson into his corner and smashed him right and left. Peter seemed a little groggy as he walked to his corner.

ROUND 17—Jackson was as fresh as a daisy, but Corbett was in just as good fettle. Sharp exchanges and short-arm blows left both blowing. They rallied nicely in a little while and Corbett's left did magnificent execution. His favorite double blow—first to the wind and then to the jaw—successfully illustrated Jackson's discomfiture.

ROUND 18—In the beginning of this round, however, Jackson was himself again and thumping at the white man's heart. To look at both men in this battle no one would ever dream that odds in betting could have been thought of before the contest. Jackson sought to regain his lost prestige in this round, but Corbett stopped all his leads with surprising cleverness and countered him once or twice on the head and over the heart. His blows seemed to lack steam, however, and did little damage. At the end of the round Corbett dealt Jackson one of the heaviest blows of the fight, a left hand swinging smash square on the mouth. Jackson was a shade wobbly at the call of time, but Corbett's efforts had told on him also, and it was still anybody's fight.

ROUND 19—Jackson, as usual, was on the aggressive, making his man back around the ring, but doing enough execution in the slapping line to prevent the Australian from taking too many privileges with his vulnerable points. The round closed with honors about evenly distributed.

ROUND 20—This was Jackson's round. He followed his man viciously, giving him no time to recover. Corbett got in a few good stops, but Jackson kept at work jabbing his left into Corbett's heart. Finally the Californian lad seemed tired of this treatment, and turning on Jackson fought him across the ring into his corner and punched him hard with both hands. Jackson escaped from chancery, and a hard and even exchange followed. Jackson was taking slightly the best of it when the gong struck.

ROUND 21—Corbett had somewhat the best of it until in closing, Jackson's left elbow caromed against Corbett's neck. It was a staggerer and Jackson had his man going for a second or two. The rebound off the ropes brought Corbett back from an awkward position to a clinch, and the most disastrous round of the fight for him to date ended.

ROUND 22—In this round Jackson continued the aggressor, and Corbett had all he could do to avoid his awful swings and dangerous jabs. It became a sort of pedestrian match around the ring, Corbett making backward and the Australian crowding him to the last limit.

ROUND 23—This was virtually a repetition of the previous one, Corbett acting as receiver-general and doing the backward pedestrian act. He looked very tired and Jackson never seemed as eager and capable. The only showing, however, that amounted to anything was interrupted by the clanging of the gong.

ROUND 24—Jackson caught the runaway once in this round and sent a hot shot into his heart region. Corbett kept out of the way after this. As surely as water dripping wears out a rock so surely did Jackson seem to be tiring

BUD RENAUD,

DUNCAN McDONALD.

Corbett into a loser. Corbett's activity of the former rounds had departed and his heart, as far as outside appearances could be judged, had gone with it. There was no fighting, but it was not the Australian's fault, Corbett refusing battle. Jackson in his usually careful style left well enough alone, and, barring his close watch on Corbett, he did not do very much more to weary him, which might involve taking chances.

ROUND 25—There was little fighting done and both men showed heavy punishment.

ROUND 26—Neither did anything remarkable, but Jackson tried time and again.

ROUND 27—Jackson forced the fighting and Corbett fought on the defensive until he managed to get in a left swing, which jarred Jackson's bowels, and Jackson's left touched up Corbett's forehead with telling effect.

A series of clinches characterized the opening of the twenty-eighth round, and in one of the breakaways Jackson dealt Corbett a fearful blow over the heart. Corbett got back with a right swing on Jackson's jaw, and a terrific fight ensued. It was stand up and give and take; it was a smashing match, and these two cleverest men in the ring to-day seemed for a time to forget their cunning. Science was left out of the question and the men banged each other might and main, each trying to get in a knock-out blow. Both were very groggy at the call of time.

When they toed the scratch for the thirty-second round they sparred for wind. Jackson got his first, and again assumed the aggressive. His leads were wild and easily avoided by his wily antagonist.

There was a sharp rally at the opening of the forty-first round, Corbett coming out second best in the exchange. Jackson evidently had held himself in reserve for a strong rib-roaster which brought Corbett to clinching tactics to save further punishment. At the end of the round in a clinch Corbett's knees seemed to weaken under him while he hung to Jackson's neck. Jackson, although far from fresh, looked much stronger than his opponent.

In the fiftieth round Corbett was plainly the weaker, Jackson was strong and confident, but his leg, injured in a recent accident, gave him considerable trouble.

In the fifty-first round both men were completely used up, and Jackson appeared to limp on the leg he sprained when thrown out of a chaise. Corbett's hands were swelled to twice their natural size, and both showed the marks of each other's handiwork.

In the fifty-fifth round Corbett landed his damaged left under Jackson's right eye, but the blow would not have dented a pincushion. Jackson countered with both hands and fought Corbett to the ropes, when the latter clinched and the round ended.

In the fifty-sixth and fifty-seventh rounds Jackson showed that he was the strongest, but little fighting was done, owing to the California Wonder being on the defensive.

In the fifty-eighth round it was evident Jackson would win, provided he had the stamina. Corbett's hands were gone by constantly coming in contact with Jackson's cocoanut, and he could not do Jackson any damage. Few blows were struck in this round or in the fifty-ninth.

In the sixtieth round when the pugilists faced each other, Hiram Cook stated both must fight and end the battle if they expected to win the $10,000. Jackson, general like, was waiting for Corbett to lead so that he would counter him, but Corbett had lost all steam and he knew he could not hurt Jackson even if he tried, owing to his hands giving him so much pain. No blows were struck although Jackson was on the *qui vive* for Corbett to lead.

The sixty-first round ended the contest. After the men faced each other Corbett's friends, who knew they had no chance to land their money, shouted make it a draw, and Corbett looked anxiously at the referee, trusting he would do so. When Jackson would advance Corbett would retreat, and these tactics were kept up until the gong sounded.

Hiram Cook, the referee, stepped to the centre of the ring, and declared that it was apparent that the men could not go on to a satisfactory finish, and, under the circumstances, he would declare it "No contest." Unless the directors of the club choose to give the men something, under the articles they signed they cannot demand a cent of the $10,000. They signed to fight to a finish, and didn't do it.

DAVE CAMPBELL.

JACK ASHTON,

Three lusty cheers were given for Corbett and three for Jackson, and the crowd filed out, but not satisfied with the ending by any means.

The battle lasted 4 hours and 3 minutes, according to POLICE. GAZETTE rules, each round lasting three minutes, not including 1 minute rest.

The purse was not divided, but the Club retained $5,000 giving the other $5,000 in equal parts to the boxers.

CHAPTER VI.

THE CORBETT AND SULLIVAN BATTLE ARRANGED.

After his battle with Jackson, Corbett returned to New York under the management of Wm. A. Brady, the popular, shrewd, energetic theatrical manager, appearing in the "Dark Secret."

On Charley Mitchell arriving in New York from England, Corbett challenged him and a match was arranged for the rival boxers to engage in a six-round glove contest, but the affair fell through.

Corbett having failed to induce any foreign champion to fight him, issued a challenge to fight John L. Sullivan, the champion pugilist of the world, for $10,000 a side, and the championship.

On February 10, 1892, William A. Brady, Corbett's manager, deposited $1,000 to bind a match with Sullivan. This was telegraphed to Sullivan, who requested his backers, Charles Johnston, of Brooklyn, and James Wakely, of New York, to cover Corbett's money,

On March 10 Wakely called at the *World* office and deposited $2,500 with the sporting editor in behalf of Sullivan. Both Corbett and Brady were out of the city, but agreed to meet Wakely at the *World* office, and post the balance of the $2,500 and sign articles of agreement.

This important proposed fistic encounter was arranged in the New York *World* office on March 15, 1892. The announcement that the match would be made attracted quite a gathering of sports, viz.: John McDonough, Phil Lynch, John Kelly, of baseball fame; John C. Humphrey, of Oakland, Cal.; Bob Smith, Billy Madden, J. C. Kennedy and James Wakely, who has made his name famous as a betting man and a plunger. The POLICE GAZETTE was represented by William E. Harding. John L. Sullivan was not present, but James Wakely attended to the matter and posted the $2,500 for the champion.

Corbett and his manager, W. A. Brady, were first on hand. Brady pulled down the $1,000 check that he had deposited a week before, and supplanted it with $2,500 in bills. As he did so, he remarked: "It was no trouble to raise this money. I could have got $10,000 as easily as this, if it had been necessary. There are men, members of high-standing clubs, right in this city, who will put up almost any amount on Corbett. I cannot use their names, as they have asked me not to; but when it comes to money we shall have all we want. I might say, also, that I have a slice of this thing myself."

Jim Wakely came along about half an hour later, and there was no time lost in opening proceedings. The first

JOHN L. SULLIVAN, EX-CHAMPION OF THE WORLD.

CHARLIE JOHNSTON, SULLIVAN'S BACKER.

question was as to a final stakeholder. Wakely said Phil Dwyer was good enough for him, but here Corbett made a manly objection.

"Mr. Dwyer would suit me in everything, and I should be glad to accept him, were it not for one consideration. He is my personal friend and has offered to back me. That he would put his money on me I know, and for that reason I cannot consent to have him as the final stakeholder. If it should happen that some question or other arises about the payment of the stakes and I should get them, everybody would say that Dwyer was prejudiced. I don't want this match to be wound up with any such feeling. I want the money to go where it belongs, without question, and I want to avoid, right now, the possibility of a question. Therefore, I object to Mr. Dwyer."

"How would Al Smith do?" asked Brady.

"Sullivan has no use for Al Smith," responded Wakely.

It is a public fact that Al Smith is not over friendly toward the big fellow, and Wakely's opposition was but to be expected.

The name of Ed. Kearney of New York came up, but Corbett did not know enough about that sporting man to accept him, and it was finally agreed to select only a temporary stakeholder, just then, and a final holder when the next deposit would be made on June 1. George N. Dickinson was accepted as temporary stakeholder of the $5,000 meantime.

The next subject was the time of fighting and the battle ground. Corbett conceded to the demand of the other side to have the fight during the first week in September. As to place, both liked New Orleans, and both agreed to give the Olympic Club of that city the preference, provided they could secure a $25,000 purse. If the Olympic Club would not hang up $25,000, then the organization that would offer the most money would get the fight. These details having been made all right all around, articles were drawn up and signed as follows :

These articles of agreement are to govern a glove contest to a finish between John L. Sullivan, champion of the world, and James J. Corbett, of California.

First—The match is to decide the heavy weight championship of the world, a stake of twenty thousand dollars ($20,000), and a purse of twenty-five thousand dollars ($25,000).

Second—The contest shall take place before the Olympic club of New Orleans, La., on Wednesday, Sept. 7, 1892. In case the said Olympic Club refuses to give a purse of twenty-five thousand dollars ($25,000), the contest shall take place before a club to be mutually agreed upon by the signers of these articles.

Third—The contest shall be under Marquis of Queensberry rules, the gloves shall be the smallest the club will allow, and other details of the contest itself shall be left to the decision of the Olympic Club or the club before which the contest shall take place. The club selected shall name the referee.

PHIL. CASEY.

BAT MASTERSON.

Fourth—The sum of twenty-five hundred dollars ($2,500) has been deposited by each party. It is agreed that the remainder of the stake of ten thousand dollars ($10,000) a side shall be deposited on the days named here—June 1, $2,500; July 10, $2,500; August 25, $2,500.

Fifth—The final stakeholder shall be agreed upon on the date of the second deposit. June 1.

Sixth—Should either party fail to comply with these articles, the money then in the hands of the temporary stakeholder shall be forfeited to the party which shall have fulfilled its obligations according to this paper.

J. C. KENNEDY,   JAMES WAKELY,
   Witness for Corbett.   For John L. Sullivan.

JOHN MCDONOUGH,   JAMES J. CORBETT.
   Witness for Sullivan.

After the match was arranged, President Charles Noel of the Olympic Club was asked how big a purse he would give and the following reply was received:

NEW ORLEANS, La., March 15.

To the Sporting Editor of the World :

Will give $25,000 for Corbett. Will mail articles to-morrow.   CHAS. NOEL.

Sullivan selected Phil Casey, the champion hand-ball player, as his trainer, and he took up his quarters at Canoe Place Inn, Good Ground, L. I. Jack Ashton also assisted in training the champion. Sullivan weighed 230 pounds when he began to train, and by constant work he reduced his weight to 210 pounds. Phil Casey was assisted toward the middle of Sullivan's sojourn at Good Ground, by Mike Cleary, who helped Sullivan to train for his fight with Jake Kilrain.

Corbett, a few weeks after the match was ratified, went into training at Deal Lake, near Asbury Park, N. J., under the management of Wm. A. Brady and Billy Delaney, well known both in New York and on the Pacific Slope as a star trainer, assisted by Jim Daly, of Philadelphia, the champion heavy-weight pugilist of Pennsylvania.

CHAPTER VII.

THE GREAT BATTLE BETWEEN CORBETT AND SULLIVAN.

The fight was decided in the Olympic Club, New Orleans, La., on Sept. 7, 1892. About 10,000 spectators witnessed it. Betting was 4 to 1 on Sullivan, 3 to 1 against Corbett.

The following is the fight by rounds:

ROUND 1—Both men were smiling. Sullivan rushed in, but missed a left-hand lead, Corbett dancing. Corbett parried a thrust and danced away again. His activity was remarkable, and the first minute was spent in sparring. The crowd began to hiss Corbett, and he continued his running tactics until half the round was over. Sullivan's

CORBETT'S TRAINING QUARTERS.

THE OLYMPIC ATHLETIC CLUB BUILDING, NEW ORLEANS, LA.

face was dark as midnight, and he seemed angry as the bell rang.   Not a blow was struck during the round.

ROUND 2—The men sparred at long range for almost a minute, Corbett dodging away every time the champion tried to force matters. He ducked a left-hand lead cleverly, but the big fellow rushed him to the ropes and caught him. Fierce fighting followed. Sullivan landed twice on Corbett's face, followed by an upper cut. Then Jim was even wilder than ever, flying about the arena like a hunted deer. Sullivan watched his chance and got in a left-hand swing, but it did not land with full force, Corbett getting back with a light punch in the belly.

ROUND 3—Sullivan missed an excellent chance, and bit his lips reproachfully. Corbett danced away from a right-hand lead at his stomach, and it was evident that he was going to make a long fight of it. John rushed in and landed lightly on the back, but it was only a glancing blow. Jim came nearer and got in a rib roaster on Sullivan's heart. Sullivan's return was short and did no damage. Corbett landed two left-hand swings on the champion's jaw, and for the first time in the fight did some work. This maddened Sullivan, who came on and got in twice on the stomach and neck without receiving a return. Corbett was astonishing the talent.

ROUND 4—The champion seemed much worried that his blows did not land, and he looked serious. Corbett's agility was remarkable. He seemed to escape Sullivan's leads with the greatest ease, but he did no work himself, and it was evident that he was playing a waiting game. His gymnastics amused the assemblage for a time. They began hissing him and cried, "Fight, fight like a man." Sullivan's leads were wild and Corbett landed lightly on the neck, the champion paying no attention to the blow. As the hissing began again Corbett came in and exchanged blows, but nothing came of it. As the fight progressed, it was painful to Sullivan's admirers to admit that he was not the champion of old, being very slow.

ROUND 5—Sullivan landed on Corbett's chest and got a counter on the neck. Corbett landed a terrific left-hand punch on the belly and followed it up with another. Then he attacked the champion savagely. Blood flew from Sullivan's eyes and nose in streams. Sullivan hugged Corbett to save himself, and Corbett pushed him away. Both men were bathed in Sullivan's blood.

ROUND 6—Corbett went at his man instantly, but a punch in the ribs stopped him, and some sparring ensued. Sullivan was weak and his face was a sight. Corbett came in and landed with the left on the stomach. In a clinch blows were exchanged, but no damage done. Both countered on the jaw and Sullivan ended it with a right-hand swing that would have ended the fight had it landed. Corbett's quickness was marvellous, and he landed his left on the broken nose at the call of time.

ROUND 7—Sullivan was strong when time was called, and walked briskly to the centre. Jim then got home a straight left on the big fellow's belly, and coming nearer

CAPT. BARRETT, OF NEW ORLEANS.

SULLIVAN RUSHES.

got three in quick succession on mouth and chin. Corbett then jabbed his left into the champion's face and the audience showed their appreciation by cheering. He landed a right-hander on the jaw. Then he rushed Sullivan to the ropes and fought him to a standstill.

ROUND 8—Sullivan attempted to force matters, landing his right heavily. Young Jim did not like this and banged the big fellow on the jaw and followed it up with another blow on the nose, getting a good stiff punch over the heart in return. Jim then punched his man twice in the ribs and got home a terrific right-hand smash on the jaw. Sullivan was weary when time was called.

ROUND 9—Sullivan's blows were short and harmless. Finally he hit Corbett on the ear, the blow sounding throughout the building. An exchange of blows followed, Sully putting his right on Corbett's ear once more. Both men clinched and the crowd shouted foul. Corbett put his left lightly on the big fellow's cheek and landed three more blows as the round ended.

ROUND 10—The men sparred warily. Sullivan put his left on Corbett's ear with force, and ducked a return in quite his old style. A strong exchange followed with honors even. Sullivan improving, he caught Corbett on the right eye, reddening the skin and making Jim knit his brows. Corbett had all the best of an exchange that followed, landing twice on the jaw.

ROUND 11—Sparring was followed by hot work, Corbett doing the most damage. Protracted sparring ensued.

The young man rushed in and had the best of a volley on the ropes. He followed it up with another smash on Sully's nose, dancing away each time out of harm's way.

ROUND 12—Corbett rained blow after blow on Sullivan's stomach, and Sullivan in attempting to escape let his guard down and received two blows on the neck and jaw. These were followed by punches in the abdomen. He played for the jaw, but missed twice and waited for an opening. He landed a terrific right-hander under Sullivan's chin, which, had it been delivered on the point of the jaw, would have ended the fight.

ROUND 13—Corbett ducked away every time Sullivan attempted to lead. Not a blow was struck until near the end of the round, when Corbett put his left on the big fellow's jaw, springing away out of danger.

ROUND 14—A sharp exchange began the battle, both landing on the jaw, and then the big fellow smashed Corbett on the cheek with his left. It made no impression on Corbett's hard face, and Jim squared matters with two punches on the mouth and chin. A sharp counter followed, both men landing with great fierceness. Corbett jabbed Sullivan on the nose and had the best of the rally that followed, his blow having more steam than Sullivan's.

ROUND 15—Each got home on the neck and jaw, and they mixed it up in lively style, Corbett doing the better work. The big fellow clinched his teeth in a vicious fashion. Corbett got home on the stomach and got away unhurt.

CORBETT LANDS ON THE STOMACH.

THEY MIXED IT UP IN LIVELY STYLE.

Sullivan's blows were weak.   Corbett's full-arm swings had a world of force.

ROUND 16—John attempted to rush in, but was met by a straight left-hander in the mouth.   Sullivan's breathing was labored, and could be heard plainly by persons twenty-feet from the ring.   Corbett punched the big fellow on the mouth and jabbed his left into the big man's stomach repeatedly, escaping punishment with ease.   They clinched, and Corbett hugged his man while the crowd yelled "foul." Corbett raised his hands deprecatingly as he broke away.

ROUND 17—There was very little fighting in this round, neither man landing a blow worthy of record.   The time was taken up in sparring, and the round was the tamest of the fight.

ROUND 18—Jim jabbed John twice in the short ribs when the big fellow atttempted to come in at the opening of the round.   Sullivan's nose had stopped bleeding, and his face was much more sightly than half an hour before. His mouth was open, for he breathed heavily.   John smashed Jim twice on the ear, but the young gladiator responded with two blows on the jaw that were scorchers. Corbett's next blow, a right-hander on the jaw, was a dangerous one, and he followed it with three more of the same kind, and Sullivan's chances waned rapidly.

ROUND 19—Corbett's cleverness in tapping Sullivan and getting away was greatly admired up to this time, and when he jabbed the big fellow four times on the face in succession the spectators raised a howl.   Sullivan here got in

his left on Corbett's breast, but it did not hu   ○or-
bett touched John L. up for two right-hande: ly,
amid more howls.   The people seemed to be ..ıuı ○orbett.

ROUND 20—Corbett fought his man to the ropes, using
his left and right on stomach and jaw.   He punished the
big man repeatedly in his wind, and it seemed to be all day
with Sullivan, who carried his right hand as though it had
been injured.   Jim jabbed the big fellow in the stomach
again and then came in, getting home on the ear and ribs
with great force.   Corbett had a marked advartage when
time was called amid deafening cheers.

ROUND 21—Corbett was out for blood and started to
finish the man who had held the championship for so many
years, and whose name was a terror to all.   He rushed in
and planted blow after blow on Sullivan's face and neck.
The champion, so soon to lose his coveted title, backed
away, trying to save himself.   He lowered his guard from
sheer exhaustion, and catching a fearful smash on the jaw,
reached to the ropes, and the blood poured down his face
in torrents and made a crimson river across the broad
chest.   His eyes were glassy and it was a mournful act
when the young Californian shot his right across the jaw
and Sullivan fell like an ox.

It was a game battle, but Sullivan was clearly out-
fought.   It was a triumph of youth, science and agility over
age and physical power.

Corbett forced the fighting from start to finish.   He
landed on Sullivan when and where he pleased.   The ex-

CORBETT LANDS ON SULLIVAN'S JAW.

SULLIVAN LANDS HIS RIGHT.

champion hit his opponent only five times altogether, and then with little force.   Sullivan's nose was broken, his face and body bruised, and he was finally battered down, a bleeding mass of humanity, unable to rise at the call of time.   Sullivan stood up against the greatest number of hard blows ever received in the ring, and showed himself to be the game man his friends knew him.   Corbett was wholly uninjured, and was as fresh as ever at the finish. Sullivan had failed to land even one of his famous lunge blows.

It was a great victory for the young Californian, who proved himself a marvel, and many an expert will admit that he made the greatest fight ever seen.

After the battle crowds assembled to greet the new champion, and even the once great John L. Sullivan's admirers cheered the tall, athletic, good looking, gentlemanly pugilist.   When Corbett reached his hotel he gave the following graphic description of his victory :

"I found Sullivan easier game than I anticipated, though I do not mean to infer by that that he is not a wonderful pugilist.   He is by far the strongest man and the hardest hitter I ever encountered, but my quickness and skill entirely nonplussed him.   I had the best of him all through. In the first place I won the toss for corners, and that annoyed him.   Then I made him go into the ring first.   He tried hard to make me do this, but I said : 'No.   He is the champion.   He challenged me.   I will follow him.' And I did.   He had to pass right by me and I was so cheerful and at ease that I could see he was wrathy.   After we got into the ring I stepped around, trying its elasticity and spring with my feet, and that disconcerted him, for he thought I would be afraid of him. When we were called to the centre of the ring to receive our instructions from the referee we were told that when ordered to 'break' we should do so at once, and not attempt to strike each other until fairly apart. 'Do you mean,' I asked, 'that we must not hit going away?'

" 'Yes,' replied Mr. Duffy.

" 'Then, suppose Sullivan hits me?' I queried.

" 'Then I will give the fight against Sullivan,' was the answer. Sullivan seemed impatient at the delay. I took hold of his hand cordially when told to shake hands, but he threw mine away disdainfully.

" In the first round I made no attempt to hit Sullivan, as I was only feeling him out. He led at me five times, but without avail. A few of his friends began to hiss, but I quieted them with a deprecatory wave of my hands.

" In the second round I began work, and I soon satisfied Sullivan that I could hit him hard and often. I smashed his nose, and after the fifth round I said to my second, Billy Delaney, 'I can knock this fellow out now,' but he begged me not to take any chances, but to bide my time. Sullivan glared at me constantly, but I only laughed at him. He called me a hard name in the eighth round, and I sailed in and smashed him right and left, body and face, until, I think, he wished he hadn't called it.

" In one of our clinches Sullivan struck me, so the next time we came together I gave him a good thump in return.

CORBETT WAS OUT FOR BLOOD.

SULLIVAN'S CHANCES WANED RAPIDLY.

As we broke apart he exclaimed, deprecatingly, 'Don't take any advantage of me!' I answered: 'I don't have to, I have you licked now.'

"I was so strong, so quick and so full of ginger all through the battle that I was surprised at myself. I never tired once, and, though men tell me that I fought faster than any one they ever saw, 1 could have kept up the pace for another hour with case.

"The gong saved Sullivan twice from being knocked out, but I did not think that the twenty-first round would end the battle when it was called. I got in three smashes on Sullivan's heart and face, and then his eyes turned up so that I could see nothing but their whites. Then I knew I had him, and I never gave him a chance to rally until he fell to the floor. I stepped back fully ten feet. I was perfectly cool and collected while he was being counted out. I was stepping forward to help him up when Billy Delaney, thinking I was excited and might hit him a foul blow, caught hold of me. I shook him off, saying : 'I know what I am about. Don't worry about me.' Then Professor Duffy tapped me on the shoulder and pronounced me the winner. I jumped forward and helped to pick Sullivan up and place him on the chair. He was unconscious and a fearful sight. They say in New Orleans that Sullivan's was the worst knock-out that ever was seen in the Olympic ring."

"I am surprised," said Corbett, "that he should be so cast down by his defeat by me. I tell you that no one can whip Sullivan who is not as fast as I am. I am not so sure that he wouldn't whip Peter Jackson, for Peter's style would suit him a good deal better than mine. Peter would go and shy with him, and no man can do that with any hope of success. From what I hear of Joe Goddard's style, I think Sullivan would lick him in three rounds."

Corbett claims a great deal of his success must be attributed to his trainer, Wm. F. Delaney, who has trained and seconded him in all his important matches.

Delaney is a fine specimen of manhood, a pleasant conversationalist and a jolly good trainer. Some of the men he has coached and trained are as follows : Young Mitchell, Tom Cleary, Jack Brady, Clarence Whistler, Herbert Slade, Mike Cleary, "Buffalo" Costello, Ed. Smith, Charley Turner and George Hammil.

Jim Corbett would trust Delaney when he would be doubtful about every other man on earth. During the great Jackson-Corbett match Delaney alone talked to Corbett, and not a word was mentioned at all until twenty rounds had been fought, and then Delaney, thinking danger was nigh, began to encourage his champion by saying : "Go cautiously, Jim, take your time, my boy; you have all night before you," etc.

CHAPTER VIII.

CORBETT'S RECEPTION IN NEW YORK.

Corbett was tendered a grand reception and welcome at Madison Square Garden, New York, September 12, 1892. Long before the doors were opened crowds filled

WM. A. BRADY, CORBETT'S MANAGER.

TRAINER DELANEY.

the streets, and great enthusiasm prevailed. After the doors were opened there was a tremendous rush.

The gathering was one of which Corbett could well be proud. There were the usual number of those intimately associated with the affairs of the squared circle, but the largest portion of the gathering was composed of business and professional men, while society was also well repre- sented. They were all there to take a look at the world's champion, and they drew a long breath of satisfaction as they gazed on the young athlete's lithe figure.

William A. Brady, Corbett's astute manager, mounted the platform. After the applause had subsided he started to make a few remarks to the spectators. He had not got past "Ladies and Gentlemen," when suddenly everybody in the Garden arose and united in a deafening yell that completely smothered Brady. The outburst was caused by the appearance of a tall young man in white trunks and green stockings, who, stripped to the waist, and with his pompadour-cut hair standing up straight and unruly, was making his way through the aisle leading from his dressing- room. It was Corbett, and he had come out before he had received the cue.

When the champion stood up in the middle of the ring and looked around, the spectators threw up their hats, waved canes, yelled themselves black in the face, and otherwise exhibited their pleasure. Dainty handkerchiefs fluttered from the boxes, while the more enthusiastic of those near the ring rushed to the ropes and tried to shake the champion's hand. Owing to the fact that his right hand was bandaged up, which was the only visible indication that he had been engaged in a desperate battle, he asked to be excused, and waved the injured member at his friends.

Corbett sat down in his corner, and Jim Daly, who had entered behind the champion, also took a seat. Then Brady held up his hand, and finally the crowd became quiet, after which he said :

"LADIES AND GENTLEMEN:—I have in my hand a letter from John L. Sullivan, who for ten years, off and on, held the title of champion of the world. On the day following Mr. Sullivan's defeat the champion sent him a note offering to spar in this place on Saturday evening. Mr. Corbett has nothing but the kindliest feeling toward Mr. Sullivan, and no one recognizes more than the new champion the sterling worth of the man whom he defeated. Mr. Corbett hopes that Mr. Sullivan's benefit will be a tremendous success. I will now read Mr. Sullivan's letter :

" ' Mr. JAMES J. CORBETT, Coleman House, City:

" ' In reply to your letter dated New Orleans, Sept. 8, 1892, will say I accept your proposition to spar at the Madison Square Garden on Saturday evening, Sept. 17. Awaiting your reply.

Respectfully,

JOHN L. SULLIVAN.' "

When Sullivan's name was mentioned there was another outburst of enthusiasm only second to that which

PRES. NOEL OF THE OLYMPIC CLUB.

VICE-PRES. SPORL OF THE OLYMPIC CLUB.

greeted Corbett's appearance, and the heartiness of the shouting showed that the big fellow is still a prime favorite with the people.

When Brady got another chance to talk, he said :

"Mr. Corbett's reply is that he will be here next Saturday night and spar at Mr. Sullivan's benefit."

Then there was more cheering, which was followed by cries of "Speech, Corbett, Speech!" When the champion heard that, he looked a trifle embarrassed, and scratched his right ear. Then he slowly arose and took a position in the centre of the ring. In a clear voice and natural manner he said :

"Ladies and gentlemen, I thank you all for your very kind reception, which I assure you I fully appreciate. I sincerely hope to see John L. Sullivan succeed in all his undertakings. I admire him very much, and will do all I can to assist him. I assure you I will do all I can to defend America in the matter of pugilism, and if I do one-half as well as John L. Sullivan has I shall be entirely satisfied."

This neat speech deepened the good opinion of the spectators and provoked more cheers. As Corbett resumed his corner a handsome floral piece was handed to him.

Then Brady introduced Mike Donovan, the friend and adviser of the champion, and the New York Athletic Club sparring instructor was heartily received. Billy Delaney, the man who trained Corbett for all his battles, next made his bow, and blushed at the thundrous applause.

After that Brady said "time," and Corbett and Daly, who had put on gloves, faced each other. Corbett's right was useless, but with his left and his expert feet he made matters very interesting for his sparring partner.   His remarkable activity, shiftiness and science were all shown in the three short rounds he sparred, and then, to a parting cheer, the young champion left the ring and pushed his way through the crowd to his dressing room.

A dense mass of people hung around the Twenty-sixth street exit until the pugilist came out to take a carriage to go to his hotel, and he received another ovation.

Since 1849 to the present time there have been many prize-ring champions of America, both foreign and native-born, but none of the famous fistic heroes ever had the opportunity of battling for the premiership of pugilism and such large purses as have been offered of late years.   Corbett has the name of fighting for the largest amount of money ever contended for in the prize ring and also the record for being the first pugilist who ever won the championship without being compelled to fight according to London prize-ring rules with bare knuckles.

Every pugilist from the time Tom Hyer flourished as champion of America in 1849 up to 1892, when James J. Corbett succeeded to the title, fought with bare knuckles and according to London prize-ring rules.   Corbett, however, entered into a contract to fight for the championship with gloves according to POLICE GAZETTE rules, with John L. Sullivan, the champion.   He won the contest and the championship of the world.

He won his spurs by his courage and determination, and wonderful activity and science, clearly demonstrating

W. D. ROSS, SECRETARY OLYMPIC CLUB.

MRS. JAMES J. CORBETT.

that he was a skillful boxer, a good general, a first-class
judge of distance, and possessed every qualification neces
sary to reign as a pugilistic champion.

CHAPTER IX.

MRS. CORBETT HAS SOMETHING TO SAY ABOUT HER HUSBAND.

Before concluding this sketch I think it appropriate to
add a chapter by Mrs. James J. Corbett, the young and
beautiful wife of the champion. Mrs. Corbett has this to
say about her husband :

" My husband's name has been so often in the newspapers and so much has been talked about him, that all this
fame he is now getting does not dazzle me as much as it
might have done otherwise. I am sure it does not turn
Jim's head in the least. Of course he is elated and so am I.
I was sure he would win and did not have much anxiety
about it until the night of the fight, and then I was a good
deal excited until the first dispatches began to come in.
When I saw how cool Jim was and was laughing every now
and then, just as I knew he laughed when he was full of
confidence, I had not a bit of uneasiness as to how the fight
was coming out.

"There has been a good deal in the newspapers about
what kind of a man Jim is—what his private character is,
and so on—and some of the things I have read did not do
him half justice, although I must say all that I have read
was very kind. Only his father and mother and his brothers and sisters and I, who have lived with him and seen

him every day in all his moods, can know what a gentle and loyal man to the very core he is.

"He and I have been married since the 28th of June, 1886, and during that time he has never been away from me longer than six weeks at a time, and from what I have noticed among other married people I do not believe many of them can say they have lived together that long and not had a cross word. Yet that is what I can say. I don't pretend to be a saint, but I don't believe any woman worthy of the name could ever be even pettish with such an even-tempered, gentle, considerate husband as mine has been to me. I spoke above about his moods. That does him an injustice. He does not have any moods. He is always just the same jolly, laughing, kind-hearted Jim. Everybody that knows him, even the little children out in San Francisco, love him. They could not do otherwise. It used to make me laugh sometimes to see him carry on with the children out there at home. When we were first married and he was a clerk in the bank they used to wait for him around the house. They knew when he was due to come home just as well as I did, and they seemed to come from all quarters to be there, and they were of all sizes, from little tow-heads to great gawky boys. Jim used to play ball with them and have all sorts of games with them, and they looked on him as just one of them. Indeed, there is an awful lot of boy in Jim and I guess there always will be, and so I have told him time and time again.

"When he was at school he did have a good many fights, and got expelled for it more than once, but it was

PROF. JOHN H. DUFFY, REFEREE.

JIM DALY, CORBETT'S SPARRING PARTNER.

always with bigger boys who were abusing the little ones. He never was quarrelsome, either as a boy or a man, but he never would stand it to see little chaps knocked about just because they were not big enough to resent it. He never had a single fight at school except for that one cause. He was always very devoted to his father and mother, and the saying that a good son makes a good husband holds good in his case anyway. Jim was brought up in the Catholic faith, and he is just as consistent in that as he is in everything else. It is his nature to be loyal and true-hearted, and I believe his faith in religion and the teachings he got in the Church had a good deal to do in making him so gentle and so fair always. Of course, he was born that way and it is his nature to have those qualities, but sometimes even persons who are by nature kind and generous have those good qualities changed by associations and they need religious belief to keep them true, although Jim's associations were always good. At any rate he is just as religious and just as attentive to his duties now that he is a man as he was when he was a boy, and no matter what comes he will always remain that way.

"I never went with Jim on but one of his trips, and then I only went part way. At the time of the Dempsey-Fitzsimmons fight in New Orleans a year ago last spring, Jim interrupted his trip to go down there and see it. Then I went to Mount Clemens, Mich., and waited for him, and when he joined me there I went on with him and finished the trip.

"Of course I am glad he has made so much money, and

I know he will never squander it, for that is not his nature. When he was a boy and began to work he always brought his earnings home and gave them to his mother, and he has always kept up thrifty habits ever since. Yet James Corbett's bitterest enemy could not say that he had a mean hair in his head. He is liberal and generous, and a man can be all that without throwing his money away foolishly, and that is where Jim has always drawn the line. Surely no woman could wish for a husband more liberal to her than mine has been to me.

"I think that Jim would rather live here in the East than in the West, and so for that matter would I. The place the papers tell about his buying down at Asbury Park is beautiful, quite out in the woods, with the lake right at the door, yet near to the railway station and to Asbury Park village. It is a lovely place to live in in the summer, but I do not think Jim would like it quite so well in the winter. I have seen it many times and always admired it, but I don't believe I either would like it so well in the winter.

"I am proud of my husband—I am willing to admit that; and any woman might well be proud of so good a one as he has been to me. I did not like his going prize-fight ing at first, and neither did his father and mother, but now that he is in it, I am proud of his success and glad to know that the success will never turn his head or make him a whit different from what he always was, and that is a manly, gentle, light-hearted man, considerate for others and true to himself and to those who love him."

THE POLICE GAZETTE

ART

OF

WRESTLING.

PROFUSELY ILLUSTRATED.

Price by Mail, Twenty-five Cents.

RICHARD K. FOX, PUBLISHER,
FRANKLIN SQUARE, NEW YORK CITY.

THE REVISED
CHAMPIONS
⇒ OF THE ⇐
AMERICAN PRIZE RING

A COMPLETE HISTORY OF THE HEAVY-WEIGHT CHAMPIONS OF AMERICA.

WITH THEIR BATTLES AND PORTRAITS; EXECUTED EXPRESSLY FOR THIS BOOK.

COMPLETE AND AUTHENTIC

THE ONLY BOOK OF ITS KIND IN THE WORLD.

PRICE BY MAIL, - 25 CENTS

RICHARD K. FOX, Publisher,
FRANKLIN SQUARE, NEW YORK.

PRIZE RING
CHAMPIONS
→→ OF ←←
ENGLAND
FROM 1789 TO 1889

PROFUSELY ILLUSTRATED

GIVING A VIVID AND GRAPHIC DESCRIPTION OF
THEIR NUMEROUS BATTLES, ALSO A BIO-
GRAPHICAL SKETCH OF EACH.

PRICE BY MAIL, - 25 CENTS.

RICHARD K. FOX, Publisher,
FRANKLIN SQUARE, NEW YORK.

BOXING

➤➤WITH➤➤

Hints on the Art of Attack and Defense

➤➤AND➤➤

HOW TO TRAIN

FOR THE PRIZE RING.

FULLY ILLUSTRATED.

BY AN EXPERT.

Price by Mail, 25 Cents.

RICHARD K. FOX, PUBLISHER,
FRANKLIN SQUARE, NEW YORK CITY.

⁜ THE ⁜
American ⁜ Athlete.

A TREATISE ON THE RULES AND PRINCIPLES
OF TRAINING FOR
ATHLETIC CONTESTS.

⤖ AND ⤖

The · Regimen · of · Physical · Culture.

⤖ ALSO ⤖

SHORT SKETCHES OF FAMOUS ATHLETES, THEIR EX-
PERIENCES, AND THE NOTABLE CONTESTS IN
WHICH THEY HAVE TAKEN PART.

FULLY ILLUSTRATED.

Price by Mail, 25 Cents.

RICHARD K. FOX, PUBLISHER.
FRANKLIN SQUARE, NEW YORK CITY,

THE

COCKER'S GUIDE

How to Train, Feed and Breed Game
Cocks for the Pit.

WITH VALUABLE HINTS, RULES AND OTHER
IMPORTANT INFORMATION.

PRICE BY MAIL, - 25 CENTS

RICHARD K. FOX, Publisher,

FRANKLIN SQUARE, NEW YORK,

Supply · and · Purchasing · Dep't.

Owing to the numerous orders I am daily receiving for all kinds of Sporting Goods and books of all descriptions, I have, for the convenience of the readers of the POLICE GAZETTE, opened a

SUPPLY AND PURCHASING AGENCY.

This department is in charge of a thoroughly competent man, and any orders that we are favored with will be filled at the manufacturers' and publishers' lowest prices. A few of the articles we refer to :

Base Balls, Base Ball Bats, Base Ball Masks, Catchers' Gloves, Breast Protectors, Lawn Tennis, Croquet, Hammocks, Fencing Foils, Fencing Masks, Ice Skates, Roller Skates, The American Hoyle, Poker Player, Hand Book of Whist, New Card Games, Hand Book of Cribbage, Progressive Poker, Pocket Hoyle, Manual of Chess, American Card Player, How Gamblers Win, One Hundred Tricks with Cards, Art of Wrestling, Boxing Made Easy, Equestrian Shirts, Jerseys, Jersey Cloth Goods (Shirts, etc.), Full Length Tights (Cotton and Silk), Knee Tights, Trunks (all colors), Leotards, Body Dresses, Bicycle Goods, Bicycle Hose, Silk Flesh Glove, English Perculine Running Pants, Improved Jock Strap, Running Shoes, Running Corks, Imported Sheffield Spikes, Seamless Shoes, Boxing Gloves, Foot Balls.

Your patronage is solicited. All orders must be accompanied by the CASH to receive attention.

$10.00 WORTH OF INFORMATION.

My NEW MAMMOTH 338-PAGE CATALOGUE of Sporting, Gymnasium, Athletic and Miscellaneous Goods, handsomely illustrated with over 1000 plates, forwarded by mail, to any address upon receipt of

Price, 25 Cents.

RICHARD K. FOX, Franklin Sq., New York.

New ✦ Cabinet ✦ Photographs.

ACTRESSES---SHOWING BUST.

Adelina Patti,
Lillian Russell,
Ida Siddons,
Amy Williams,
Maud Stuart,
Elsie Cameron,
Miss Jerome,
Helen Dacre,
Belle Archer,
Lurline Birdsall,
Edith Chester,
Helen Barry,
Anna Colwell,
Leslie Chester,
Jennie McNulty,
Edith Merrill,
Marie Tempest,
Miss Engle
Pearl Ardine
Mlle. Bado
Mlle. De Marsy
Lizzie Fleury
Violet Cameron,
Pauline Lucca
Louise Thorndyke
Emma Nevada
Mlle. Eames,
Mlle. Nullijji,
Mlle. Paulette,
Mlle. Carmesi,
Mlle. Lehure,
Mlle. Fa Beauty,
Mlle. Debarcourt,
Mlle. Dieroza,
Mlle. Dandeville,
Mlle. Chossaing,
Mlle. Lhery (4),
Mlle. Coburc,
Emma Carson,

Clara Morris,
Annie Walters,
Carrie Wilson,
Helen Weathersby,
Lizzie Fletcher,
Lelia Farrell,
Frankie Kemble (2),
Louise Kerker (2),
Agnes Evans,
Cora Tinnie,
Marion Percy,
Corinne,
Judic,
Ada Rehan,
Lilly Post,
Letty Lind,
Miss Parr,
Emily Rigl,
Miss Bice,
Miss Elvin,
Mrs. Haner,
Amy Rocha,
Cornalba,
Lilia Blow,
Eva Lee,
Annie Robe,
Annie Irish,
Lotta,
Janisch,
Alice Evans,
Miss Parrice,
Emma Gaie,
Sylvia Grey,
Miss Mack,
Sadie Martinot,
Clara Louise Kellogg,
Fanny Davenport,
Mrs. Langtry,
Minnie Maddern,

Isabelle Urquhart,
Maggie Arlington,
Georgia Cayvan,
Neda Bowers,
Maggie Mitchell,
Minnie Palmer,
H. Dauvray Ward,
Maude Wentworth,
Adelaide Emerson,
Florence St. John,
Maud Harrison,

Mrs. Fitzherbert,
Geraldine Ulmer (2),
Phyllis Broughton,
Florence Ashbrooke,
Irene Verona (2),

Fay Templeton,
Marion A. Erie,
Lillie May Hall,
Agnes Miller,
Florence Miller,
Etta Martens (2),
Laura Russell,
Marion Roberts,
Hope Eytinge,
Maude Granger,
Kate Forsythe,
Lillian Grubb,
Julia Marlowe,
Ada McDonald,
Miss Crouzet,
Estelle Clayton,
Miss Van Osten,
Isabella Evesson,
Miss Sardtat,
Flora Henderson,
Pauline Hall,
Mollie Fuller,
Selina Fetter,
Sturgis Leath,
Miss Brewster,
Marie Jansen,
Cora Tanner,
Jane Hading,
Louise Lester,
Louisa Dillon,
Lillian Olcott,
Marie Halton,
Rose Newham,
Mabel Millette,
Bell Howard,
Josephine Cameron,
Grace Stewart,
Miss Raymond,
Clara Dervyra,

Rosina Vokes (2),
Annie Meyers,
Maude Branscombe
Marion De Grey
Duchess of Leinster
Lillian Price
Agnes De LaPorte
Marion Edgecombe
Mlle. Dauvray
Miss Tua
Mrs. Scott Siddons
Emma Thursby
Kate Davis
May Wheeler (2),
Ella Wentnerbee,
Marie Prescott,
Katherine Lynn,
Bella Raymond,
Mrs. L. Eldridge,
Miss Fortescue,
Florence Dysart,
La Belle Fatima,
Harriet Vernon,
Marion Hood,
Sara Holmes,
Isabelle Coe,
Xenia Carlstadt,
Hilda Thomas,
Mlle. Darcelle
Maude Millett,
Mrs. Marini
Mrs. Barrington
Miss McNulty
Corine Gilchrist
Mlle. Vallier.
Carrie Godfrey,
Josie Mansfield
Mlle. Bertini
Flora Moore,

ACTRESSES---IN TIGHTS.

Pauline Markham,
Anna Boyd (3),
Clara Terry
Ruth Stetson (2),
Mabel Mitchell,
Miss Bell,
Carrie Evlyn,
Effie La Tour,
Elsie Gerome,
Amy Gordon,
Daisy Murdock (2),
Grace Seavey,
Annie Summerville,
Fanny Rice,
Jessie West,
Alice Arnold,

May Bell,
Elaine Carringford,
Gracie Wilson,
Annie Sutherland (2),
Miss Valles,
Mlle. Debnege,
Miss Spiller,
Grace Huntley
Jennie Lee
Victorina
Ida Yearntce,
Miss Miller,
Jeannette Larger,
Abelania Barrason,
Irene Verona (5),
Sylvia Grey,

Emma Carson,
Maude Granger,
Carrie Wilson,
Leila Farrell (2),
Agnes Evans,
E. Verge (2),
Lillian Grubb,
Flo Henderson,
Ada Webb,
Nellie Farren.
Miss Stuard (4),
Harriet Vernon,
Addie Conyers,
Mlle. Dieroza,
Mlle. Volti,
Billie Barlow,

Mlle. Bhanra,
Miss Valles
Mlle. Ferrare
Miss Sheridan
Florence Girard,
Carrie Andrews (2),
Genevieve Brett,
Hattie Delaro,
Vernona Jarbeau,
Theodora Detillbert
Louise Montague,
Florence Chester
Laura Burt,
Lilly Elton (4),
Marion Elmore,
Ella Moore,

Kate Uart (2).
Miss Robinson,
May Livingston,
Kitty Wells,
Alice Townsend,
Mlle. Germaine,
Marion Manola,
Miss Pohak,
Mlle. Duprey,
Eliza Vovel,
Miss Venus,
Eunice Vance
Annie Bennett

ACTRESSES---IN COSTUME.

Lydia Thompson,
Mary Anderson,
Margaret Mather,
Mrs. J B. Potter (2),
Maggie Cline,
Isabella Irving,
Myra Goodwin,
Katie Seymour,
Rose Coghlan
Minnie Jeoffreys,
Catherine Lewis
Jennie Winston,
Amelia Glover,
Mrs. J W Florence,
Annie Pixley,
Theo.
Georgie Dennin,
Madame Gerster,
Modjeska,

Kate Claxton,
Clara Thorpe,
Adelaide Detchon,
Fannie Bloodgood.
Amorita Bonfinella.
Emily Darrou.
Mlle. Franchiln
Surf Queen
Laura Don
Mrs. A. Nellson
Mrs. Chanfrau
Bertha Ricci
Paola Marie
Irene Verona.
Isabel Urquhart,
Maude Stewart,
Marion Elmore,
Helen Barry,
Mlle. Theiry,

Marie Finney,
Sybil Sanderson,
Mrs. Kendal,
Alice Lethbridge,
Marion Hood,
Mrs Bernard Beere,
Maude Richardson,
Mlle. Perlane,
Mlle. Tanzi,
Mlle. Ajour,
Mdle. Pauline.
Mlle. Grigolatis,
Mlle. Carmen.
Mlle. Nerette,
Marie Cahill,
Belle Bilton,
Zelda De Lussan,
Jennie La Tellier,
Sylvia Gerrish,

Mlle. Bonnet (2)
Rose Murray
Pearl Eytinge
Marie Roze
Agnes Booth
Christine Nillson
Emma Juch
Mary Moore
Ella B. Sheridan,
Ellen Terry,
Della Ferrell,
Carrie Tu Tein,
Mabel Hudson,
Marion Pierce,
Miss Williamson
Marie Wainwright,
Sara Bernhardt,
Lorta,
Pauline Hall,

Sadie Martinot,
Minnie Palmer,
Lillian Russell,
Modjeska,
Clara Morris,
Helen Weathersby,
Marie Jansen,
Marie Halton (2),
Dollie Noble,
Adelaide Fitz Allen,
Jeannette Bouveret,
Minnie Dupree,
Miss Dunscombe
Soledad Menendez
Mlle. Stewen
Jennie Hauk
Jeffreys Lewis
Mattie Vickers
Emma Abbott

Lightning Source UK Ltd.
Milton Keynes UK
UKHW022154050922
408362UK00006B/1417

9 780343 313364